Cool & Calm Coloring for Kids

Illustrations by Stéphanie Rousseau

My Mandalas

BARRON'S

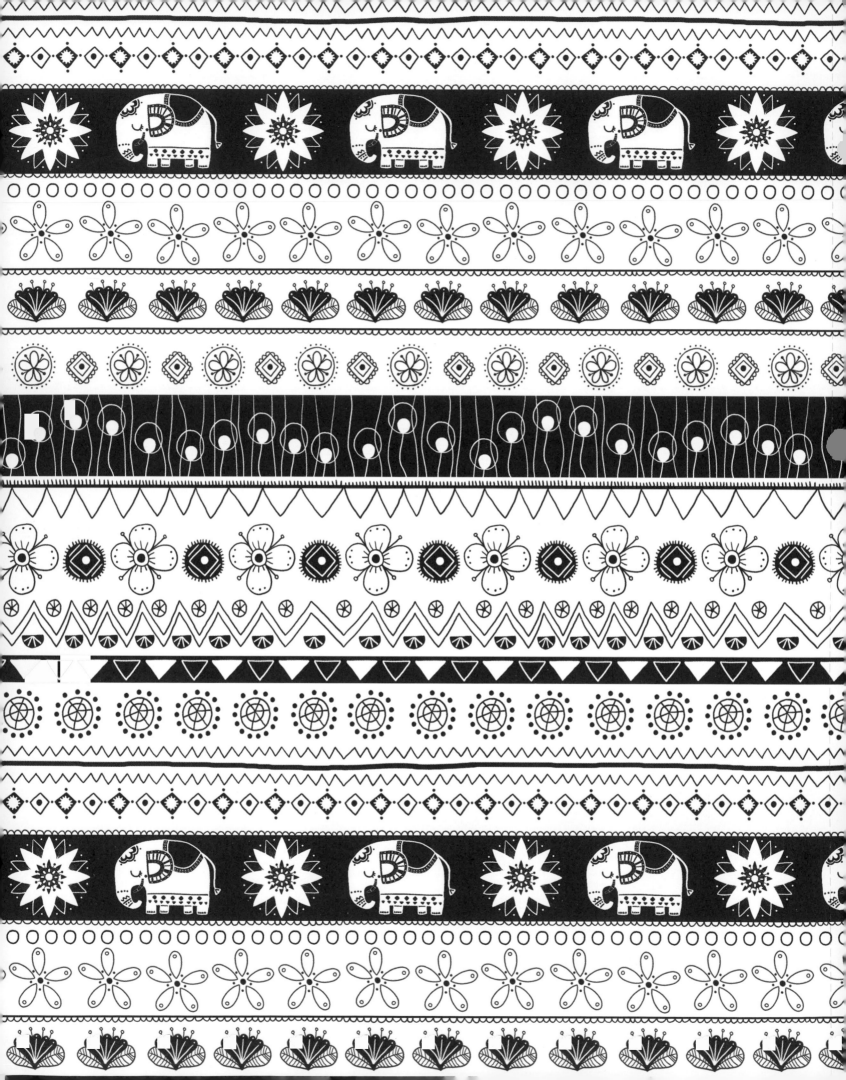

Published in the French language originally
under the title: **Mes mandalas**
© 2015, Éditions Gründ, an imprint of Édi8, Paris

First edition for North America published in 2016 by Barron's Educational Series, Inc.

All inquiries should be addressed to:
Barron's Educational Series, Inc.
250 Wireless Boulevard
Hauppauge, New York 11788
www.barronseduc.com

ISBN: 978-1-4380-0884-4

Date of Manufacture: February 2016
Manufactured by: Leo Paper Group, Heshan, China

Printed in China

9 8 7 6 5 4 3